The Fourth
Monkey

The Fourth Monkey

POETRY WITH A PURPOSE

Lakshmy Menon Chatterjee

PARTRIDGE
A Penguin Random House Company

ISBN: Hardcover   978-1-4828-3882-4
             Softcover   978-1-4828-3881-7
             eBook   978-1-4828-3883-1

To order additional copies of this book, contact
Partridge India
000 800 10062 62
orders.india@partridgepublishing.com

www.partridgepublishing.com/india

Contents

To my parents, my husband, Sid,
and my daughter, Anju.

About The Book

The Fourth Monkey is a collection of poems that represents Lakshmy's thoughts, observations, frustrations, and inspirations, derived from everyday life. All her poems deal with realism or pseudo-realism, whether these are social issues, relationships, or nature. She hopes that these poems will have a positive impact and create awareness on the myriad of problems that affect today's population. The title of this book, The Fourth Monkey, is also the title of one of her poems in this collection, and more or less encompasses the underlying theme of this book. Lakshmy wants her poems to resonate with her readers so that they are able to appreciate and understand the words that they read. Every poem in this collection has a purpose, whether it is to speak up against archaic beliefs or unjust practices, contemplate on the complications of relationships or life, or simply appreciate nature's bounty and the other good things life has to offer. She wants her poems to offer hope in the face of adversity. The paintings and photos contained in this book are also produced by Lakshmy.

Some of the events described in her poems are based on facts. But all the names of people used in this book are purely fictional and any resemblance to people, alive or dead, is purely coincidental.

APPRECIATION

For I Am She

Amber eyes ablaze,
Beauty with grace,
Menacing if angry,
Wild and carefree.

Munificent nature,
Majestic creature,
Saunters in pride,
Honest, dignified.

Devoted to friends,
Dreadful to fiends,
Loyal to her mate,
Royalty incarnate.

Ever doting mother,
Resolute protector,
Bound by her duty,
Leonine, for I am she.

Lioness And Cub
(Photo Credit - Lakshmy Menon Chatterjee)

Scent of Happiness

Ah, that delightful scent,
What could it be?
Enveloping the environment,
With its sweet earthy
Perfume that the
Wind has spread.
All around.
Is it from the sky? Instead,
Is it from the ground?
It invigorates,
It spreads happiness,
What could be the reason?
And then I realize,
It is the first raindrop
After a long, dry season!

To Our Fallen Patriots

A life of many great battles,
Fought with courage and valor.
Now honored with hundred bugles,
And burning incense of myrrh.

A life spent in selflessness,
In defense of one's country.
Now lost in eternal darkness,
Just a photo in the gallery.

A life where duty came first,
Duty to your beloved nation.
Your comrades have dispersed,
But they salute your devotion.

A life lost quite prematurely,
Before the birth of your sons.
Hopes snuffed out customarily,
Remembered with upraised guns.

These lost lives we will honor,
As citizens of an indebted nation.
We shall speak up with candor,
Your sacrifices never forgotten.

The Greatest Ship

Like roaring turbines
That move great bodies,
It has the power
To make disparate minds
Move as one.

Like a steady rudder
That gives direction,
It guides people
To open minds and
Think differently.

Like a beacon of light
That provides safe passage,
It illuminates the path
To happiness for those who
Lose their way.

Like the sturdy hull
That unites its occupants,
It creates a bond
So special and strong that
Transcends mundane emotions.

Like the majestic ship
That connects nations,
It connects friends
With different goals who
Share a passion.

Lakshmy Menon Chatterjee

A Moment of Happiness

Those eyes, once alive and joyful,
Now look so vacant.
That face, once so beautiful,
Is now wrinkled and decadent.
There are more faces like this,
With eyes that long for affection.
Their only fault lies in this,
That old age is their affliction.
Do not forget their contribution,
Do not forget their kind-heartedness,
Do not engage in retribution,
Against those who once gave you happiness.
They may have their limitations,
But, remember they cared and clothed you,
Fed you, when they went through deprivations.
Remember, that someday you will be old too.
Let us do a good deed,
And give them our hands to clasp,
In their time of need,
When they breathe their last gasp.

Blessed

Like the dependable wings of a butterfly,
That finally breaks out from its cocoon,
With life's many struggles blessed am I,
Stronger am I like a battle-worn platoon.

There are many disagreements in my family,
And there are many emotions running deep,
Blessed am I with that which completes me,
My family, like a shepherd's flock of sheep.

Some complain about the heat of the summer,
And for some, the winter cold is agonizing,
Blessed are we to enjoy seasons of colors,
To celebrate the visual joy that they bring.

So many in the world who die of starvation,
Multitudes who lose their lives in warfare,
Blessed are we who have enough of nutrition,
Blessed are we to be alive without despair.

Death and sickness can dampen your spirit,
The loss of loved ones can break your heart,
Blessed am I to be strong, healthy, and fit,
Blessed am I to have loved before I do depart.

Unconditional

Your big brown eyes melt my worries away,
Your faith in me keeps my fears at bay.

You unabashedly love me with your heart,
My harsh words sometimes tear you apart.

You show affection in more ways than one,
You keenly await me when my day is done.

You sense when I am in danger before I do,
You keep me company when friends bid adieu.

You know when I am sad and give me my space,
When I am tired, you gently slacken your pace.

You love to walk by my side in the morning,
You wait for these moments with such longing.

You only need my hands to lovingly hug you,
Maybe a special treat or a big bone to chew.

You wag your tail whenever I call your name,
Your loyalty can put human beings to shame.

Unconditional love is what you always show,
My shining beacon that will always glow.

No wonder they call you a man's best friend,
We will be there for each other till the end.

Attention Monger
(Photo Credit: Lakshmy Menon Chatterjee)

Dilemma of Desires

You stood there smugly,
A dark, brooding picture
Of immaculate sensuality.

Our gazes met briefly,
Mutually appraising the
Possibilities of a romance.

My heart fluttered wildly,
Composure falling asunder
As you stepped towards me.

You smiled charmingly,
Looking straight through me
As you waved at somebody.

I looked away awkwardly,
Feeling extremely foolish for
Having assumed a dalliance.

I regarded you longingly,
Hoping for another chance to
Rekindle our brief fascination.

You turned to me briefly,
Bestowing me a knowing glance
And a sigh for what was not to be.

This dilemma of desire sadly,
Will remain with you forever
As you accompany another.

The Class Reunion

Memories of good old times,
Return as the clock chimes.
Anticipation infuses moods,
Assuming changed attitudes.

Old friends, bygone rivals,
Some unknown, amid arrivals.
Older facades, some scarred,
Some just put up a charade.

Recollecting funny stories,
From vaults of our memories.
Sharing life's happenings,
Some sorrows and blessings.

Some pretensions do unfold,
Some bitterness is cajoled.
But the mood is quite joyful,
And the chitchat is playful.

Then comes time for photos,
All try to smile and pose.
When the event winds down,
We all prepare to leave town.

Lakshmy Menon Chatterjee

Until we meet another time,
I recall this day sublime.
Social media will reconnect,
Bonds I want to resurrect.

Natural Alchemy

Nature's mystic potion,
Sets alchemy in motion.
Green leaves turn gold,
Autumn's tendrils unfold.

The cool nip in the air,
Makes goose bumps flare.
The aroma of apple pies,
Fills the air with sighs.

Leaves float in abandon,
Where the winds beckon.
A blanket of auburn hues,
Embodies Earth's refuse.

Farmers reap the yields,
Remaining in the fields.
Animals collect the rest,
To survive winter's test.

The trees now lay bare,
Crooked limbs they wear.
They shudder in the wind,
As autumn sprigs rescind.

Golden environs dissipate,
As winter enters the gate.
Nature adopts a new color,
As the breeze gets colder.

Bared (Photo Credit: Lakshmy Menon)

That House On Binza La Belle

Childhood memories are capricious,
Some of them stay with you forever,
And some dissipate quickly like dew.

And some remain forgotten, ignored,
Until a vision ignites those embers,
Sparking a bonfire of feelings anew.

That painting of a house on a hill,
Triggered a memory that lay hidden,
Of a house that offered a lovely view.

I pictured my home on Binza La Belle,
A big, white house with inner light,
Under a bright sky of cerulean blue.

I remembered the wild pumpkin patch,
That kindly grew in our modest lawn,
Out of which my mother made a stew.

It was the first time to be witness,
To the countless abundance of nature,
And having the luck to taste it too.

The other memory was of a mother cat,
Who found shelter on our front porch,
Feeling secure to give birth in our milieu.

The kittens were an absolute delight,
Little impish fur balls of friskiness,
Being my friends until they bid adieu.

But my most unforgettable memory was,
Of the verdant valley that lay before,
And the scent of roses that did imbue.

That house on Binza La Belle had magic,
Its every nook and corner I remembered,
Even if my memories of this home are few.

CONTEMPLATION

Liberating Skeletons

You are the troubled master,
Of a heavy and dark closet,
Unlocked it has been never,
If opened, can never be shut.

There are truths that reside,
Things you have left hidden,
No one has ever looked inside,
This closet, known to only one.

But this closet is now full,
Bursting at its weak hinges,
It is now time to be truthful,
And cross over a few bridges.

Have no fear my dear friend,
For this is who you truly are,
Reveal, so that you can mend,
And clear away that ugly scar.

Let the sunlight filter in,
Let the shackled skeletons go,
Accept you have done no sin,
And your true self will show.

Many may not readily accept,
This skeleton you have shown,
Remember how much you wept,
Before reaching this milestone.

Know this, that love is universal,
Be it for the opposite or same,
It is as pure as a white crystal,
There is no need for any shame.

Mirrors Do Lie

This reflection in the shiny mirror,
This is what the world normally sees.
Nobody bothers to look a little deeper,
To follow my soul's inner mysteries.

This reflection repeats my spoken words,
This is what the world normally hears.
If only thoughts could hold big placards,
Would the world understand my lone tears.

This reflection mimics my wanton actions,
This is what the world normally judges.
If only these emotions came with captions,
Against me would there be less grudges.

This reflection is sometimes too unkind,
This is what the world normally believes.
If only the world was not so wholly blind,
They would know how this mirror deceives.

My Rose-Tinted Glasses

'What you see is not what you always get,
Do not believe,' my mother had always said,
But I could foresee better than many others,
My counsel was far sounder than my mother's.

I know that we may not get all that we want,
I certainly do not consider myself a savant,
But I knew my heart was in the right place,
I just wanted to create my own special space.

When I was derided for the choices in my life,
I stood by my decisions in the face of strife,
'The proof is in the pudding,' as wise men say,
I stand vindicated to the eve of this fine day.

There is one secret about me that nobody knows,
I use rose-tinted glasses when days are morose,
They help me envision what others cannot grasp,
They forever reside with me in my mind's clasp.

Now that my secret is revealed to one and all,
Change the color of your vision to stand tall,
Even when you wade through the depths of misery,
You only own the power to be happy and carefree.

You can borrow the rose-tinted glasses anytime,
It will help you protect your vision from grime,
When you are feeling despondent, down, or blue,
Tell me your problems and I promise to save you.

The Fourth Monkey

Three wise monkeys carved on an olden door,
Knowledge handed down from ancient folklore,
Proclaimed, 'See, speak, hear evil no more,'
But I seek the wisdom of monkey number four.

Confucius, the learned one, spoke of propriety,
A code of conduct for the meek and the mighty,
A lesson spurring mankind towards more sobriety,
He spoke of four tenets of the utmost gravity.

The fourth one, lost in the annals of history,
Its teachings, forever remained a deep mystery,
If known, would have foiled the wicked savagery,
That haunts our past and events contemporary.

For the fourth monkey had true wisdom to share,
It implored mankind to never react to a dare,
Or act in any manner to abuse or willfully scare,
Had this been known, there would be no warfare.

Truth is, nobody remembers the ancient doctrines,
Crafted wisely through our civilization's origins,
Perhaps monkeys, historically our distant cousin,
Can remind mankind to stop behaving like vermin.

Let us add that fourth monkey to the olden door,
To give company to the three monkeys from before,
Come, let us again revive this ancient folklore,
So mankind will neither do nor say evil no more.

The Fourth Monkey - Watercolor Painting
By Lakshmy Menon Chatterjee

The Story After

The culmination of every tale,
Always left us in blissful rapture.
The story that they never unveil,
The story beyond happily ever after.

For life is not a bed of roses,
Nor is it a walk in the park.
Misunderstandings between spouses,
Expectations remain in the dark.

Love bonds lonely hearts as one,
But lapses in the union of minds.
Once the deal is sealed and done,
The stark reality slowly unwinds.

Love makes you blind as they say,
Marital bliss is mostly seasonal.
Sometimes good, sometimes a bad day,
But hope for serenity is eternal.

Happily ever after may not exist,
The story may not always be pleasant.
Rays of sunlight can penetrate the mist,
And not lead to an annulment.

Never give up, fairy tales are unreal,
The deal was for worse or for the better.
Even if the situation is not ideal,
This is the pledge you made at the altar.

The Value of Nothing

When you have nothing to worry about,
You have everything to be happy for.
When you have nothing to speak aloud,
You will value silence a little bit more.

When you choose to desire nothing more,
You will value the destiny that you pursue.
When you know there is nothing to abhor,
You will realize that hatred has no value.

When fear is no longer a viable choice,
You value the battles that you can deal.
When there are no more opinions to voice,
You will value the convictions you feel.

When people's words no longer ring true,
You will value the honesty of your being.
When you possess nothing of real value,
You will understand the value of nothing.

Unapologetic

Perfection is for the Gods,
But I am just human;
Accept my shortcomings,
Because I am unapologetic.

Beauty is for pictures,
But I am just human;
Appreciate my wrinkles,
Because I am unapologetic.

Curiosity is for house cats,
But I am just human;
Believe in my apathy,
Because I am unapologetic.

Traditions are for society,
But I am just human;
Encourage my individuality,
Because I am unapologetic.

Strength is for the wind,
But I am just human;
Respect my frailty,
Because I am unapologetic.

Apologies are for the guilty,
But I have done no wrong;
Let me be as I am,
Because I am unapologetic.

The Feather On My Shoulder

Today, as I walked through memory lane,
I observed a black feather on my shoulder.
Stiff and unyielding, it looked fairly arcane,
What it meant, I just could not remember.
And then I noticed at the tip, a red stain,
A flood of images insinuated the answer.
A memory broke through this haze of pain,
'Twas hidden deep in my mind's blotter.
Confused I was, and I wanted to stay sane,
But curiosity was urging me to dig deeper.
I then decided to not waste my time in vain,
Because the answer really did not matter.
I knew my past needs to drown in the drain,
So that my future life can be much brighter.

Unrequited Love

My first real crush,
Although not the last.
Memories dart in and out,
Of my feelings unprofessed.

When you were nearby,
My heart fluttered.
My thoughts confused,
Your every word caressed.

We were adolescents,
Our hearts unscarred.
My heart was yours,
But you never guessed.

Great friends we were,
Though we were different.
Our faiths, dissimilar,
Divergent ideas expressed.

Love would not endure,
If it was reciprocated.
Best it remained unrequited,
And in me forever repressed.

You are just a footnote,
In my history of past loves.
You may no longer be around,
But with true love I am blessed.

The Phoenix Within

I awoke in abysmal darkness,
Clawing for my passage out.
But the journey was endless,
With no one to hear me shout.

I knew not this gloomy cell,
Although it looked familiar.
My very own morsel of hell,
Encountering my doppelganger.

We dueled a battle of minds,
Brightness against obscurity.
I wanted to burn the blinds,
And escape this dark cavity.

I fought long and gallantly,
Against my mighty alter ego.
My future would be ghastly,
If forfeiture were to follow.

I looked deep within myself,
And discovered the phoenix.
Rising out of ashes itself,
To battle with our nemesis.

We were more than a match,
My doppelganger succumbing.
We locked it under a latch,
To prevent another uprising.

A phoenix resides within all,
Emerging when you need succor.
Never give in, ever stand tall,
You are your very own savior.

Necessity for Chaos

Caste quells equality,
It is not a necessity.

Rivalry spawns enmity,
It is not a necessity.

Media wrecks morality,
It is not a necessity.

Politics ruin honesty,
It is not a necessity.

Glut fosters docility,
It is not a necessity.

Wisdom buoys diversity,
It is now a necessity.

Poverty needs charity,
It is now a necessity.

Thoughts need brevity,
It is now a necessity.

War would bring unity,
It is now a necessity.

Chaos incites clarity,
It is now a necessity.

Final Call

Most people dread me.

Some greet me freely.

I destroy to create.

Never do I negotiate.

Resulting from life,

The end of any strife.

I am the omnipresent,

Purveying each judgment.

No one can ever escape,

My dark cloak and cape.

I cannot be imprisoned,

I am rarely emblazoned.

I am a relief to some,

Whose life is a chasm.

My methods do differ,

But I never ever err.

When you have lost all,

You await my final call.

Wondering who I may be?

I am one no one can see.

Melody of Maladies

Maladies of the human psyche,
Seven of them are noteworthy.
These seven are quite deadly,
As told in Dante's allegory.

The first of these was lust,
It could forever wreck trust.
Relationships could go bust,
Making hearts turn callused.

Gluttony and its cousin greed,
Always wrapped in wanton need.
The things they wanted varied,
But it was extravagant indeed.

Sloth, the next deadly malady,
Defined by absolute inactivity.
Necessity is the single remedy,
To be divested from the apathy.

Envy and wrath go hand in hand,
One leads, the other is behind.
But wrath has its own command,
Not requiring envy beforehand.

Pride always precedes a fall,
The final malady of them all.
Pride never allows the gall,
To apologize for staying tall.

But, if the maladies went away,
No one would meditate or pray.
Virtue would have naught to say,
Life would be morose and gray.

Fields of Sunshine

Dreading the arduous drive,
Shifting to a strange place,
Seeking a different life,
Beginning a fresh phase.

Driving past dull cities,
Blazing heat on my face,
Inhaling the dusty breeze,
Leaving a memory trace.

Moving along open plains,
Cherishing nature's bounty,
Observing grimy bylanes,
Defining this tiny county.

Chancing upon this field,
Shining like mottled gold,
Beckoning me to just yield,
Appealing to be extolled.

Interrupting this journey,
Stopping my car alongside,
Walking through shrubbery,
Feeling slightly stupefied.

Stroking velvet sunflowers,
Pausing to breathe the air,
Searching for some answers,
Sending a solitary prayer.

Hearing the flowers speak,
Murmuring a soothing tune,
Asking me to not be weak,
Lulling me into a swoon.

Thanking them for wisdom,
Sensing peace within me,
Feeling no longer glum,
Proceeding to my destiny.

Be My Turtle Dove

We stood by each other,
Through thick and thin.
You were my only anchor,
Protecting me from sin.

Thru our companionship,
At times, we were alone.
Hurdles in a relationship,
Can rip like a cyclone.

Whenever I contemplate,
I remember great days.
You were my soul mate,
Memories I cannot erase.

Now you seem so distant,
Not choosing to share.
Love seems to be absent,
I feel you do not care.

You always wear a frown,
Finding fault with me.
Egging me for a showdown,
Making me feel guilty.

Let us take a step back,
And revive our affection.
Let us take another crack,
At fixing this affliction.

We can attempt to revive,
Our commitment and love.
I wish you would strive,
To be like a turtle dove.

Turtle doves form a bond,
That lasts till their end.
Let our love correspond,
So our hearts can mend.

Footprints On The Shore

I was walking along the shore,
Sand crusting around the feet,
Many lovely memories I adore,
Revived to life as they fleet.

I looked back along the trail,
And noticed unusual footprints,
In size, not of similar scale,
But still, these were imprints.

Curiosity got the better of me,
Coming back the way I had gone,
I studied my footprints closely,
And found they were not my own.

I did not understand the magic,
Or the science of this mystery,
The meaning was quite cryptic,
Taking me back into my history.

Then a baritone voice declared,
'Fear not dear child, it is me,
The path you walked was shared,
And those tracks belong to me.'

Lakshmy Menon Chatterjee

I asked him the meaning of this,
And he told me he had followed,
For his steps, I will not miss,
Whenever mine were swallowed.

'Your travel will not be easy,
And you may not always be right,
But I stand by you to foresee,
And show you the path of light.'

'And when hope seems misplaced,
And the way ahead looks bleak,
You can have my steps retraced,
And choose the path you seek.'

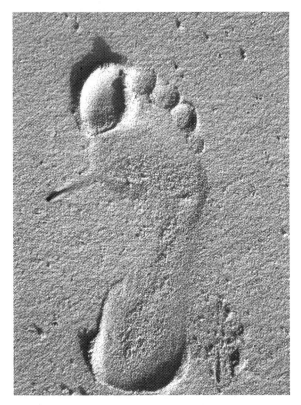

Footprints (Photo Credit: Lakshmy Menon Chatterjee)

Surreptitious Seduction

You pin me with your penetrating gaze,
Undressing me inch by agonizing inch.
I feel a deep ache coursing through me,
Setting me on a path of self-destruction.
You are going to be my ultimate nemesis,
Sucking my very being with just your eyes.
You then grace me with a provocative grin,
Shredding the last remnants of my defense.
My knees seem to have lost their senses,
Forcing me to lean against some support.
You walk towards me slowly and confidently,
Like how a predator approaches its prey.
Like a deer frozen in oncoming headlights,
I watch you in fascination and trepidation.
You close in, your masculine scent stronger,
And then you place your finger under my chin.
You let your finger slowly trace my contours,
Urging my body to arch against your frame.
I cannot resist, I surrender to your caress,
Pining for more as you relentlessly arouse me.
I whimper with pleasure, seeking much more,
I give in, begging you to take me as you will.
But you just play with me, stoking my desire,
Without making the move for the prized kill.
You now know that I am your prisoner forever,
Until you consume the center of my essence.

This knowledge gives you the vital advantage,
And you surreptitiously extricate yourself.
I will you to stay, to hold me, to touch me,
But you will not give yourself up so easily.
This is just a teaser you explain patiently,
For the seduction you have planned in detail.
I let you go assured about our upcoming tryst,
Until then, I relive these passionate seconds.

Roses Are Not Always Red

Differences makes life interesting,
Making memories more captivating.

'Tis the reason opposites attract,
Keeping such relationships intact.

While the sun provides the light,
The moon brightens up the night.

Fire burns everything in its wake,
And ice can heal you from an ache.

While sweets can give you a high,
Bitterness surely makes you cry.

The rose thorns can make you hurt,
Whereas roses can help you flirt.

Let us learn to welcome diversity,
So from envy and hate we are free.

Coloring our lives with tolerance,
Would brighten up our conscience.

There is more beauty in variety,
Than you will find in uniformity.

It's why roses are not always red,
Blooming in varied colors instead.

Monochromatic Hearts

Race, color, caste, and creed,
You are defined by your deed.

Religion, cult, and tradition,
The cause of so much tension.

Christian, Hindu, Muslim, Jew,
It's time to bid enmity adieu.

Wealthy, middle-class, and poor,
Money prompts much heartsore.

Fair, dark, brown, or yellow,
Skin color makes you the foe.

Color and race do not matter,
One cannot trump the other.

So, whenever you feel acerbic,
Know hearts are monochromatic.

If hearts are of the same color,
Why cannot we become better?

Hopes For India

I hope to experience a much safer India,
Where women can live and breathe bravely.
I hope to realize a much braver India,
That can take on challenges fearlessly.
I hope to develop a more fearless India,
Eradicating any anarchy systematically.
I hope to build a more systematic India,
Where law and order work as one perfectly.
I hope to live in a picture-perfect India,
Where life can be lived in good harmony.
I hope to sustain a more harmonious India,
Where all religions can coexist peacefully.
I hope to promote a more peaceful India,
Where disputes are resolved amicably.
I hope to foster a more amicable India,
That can lead other countries decisively.
I hope to represent a more decisive India,
That will become a superpower ultimately.
These are my hopes for my beloved India,
Dreams that would be achieved hopefully.

Paper Boats

Reds, whites, yellows, and blues,
Paper boats floating in many hues.
Some are big, and some are small,
They are flowing to their downfall.

When paper boats are set to sail,
There is hope, they would not fail.
They twist, turn, and twirl around,
Like a ballerina who is spellbound.

The brook lights up like a rainbow,
As more boats drift down the flow.
Though their purpose stays unknown,
Like lost gems from a vacant throne.

They all carry an identical message,
To survive these rites of passage.
Their destination remains the same,
Their voyage is their claim to fame.

For it is the journey that decides,
Which boat will survive the tides.
Not every boat is of similar paper,
Some boats are tougher and braver.

The boats that achieve their goals,
Are those that reach their shoals.
Even if their journey was difficult,
They have stories on which to exult.

When The Clouds Gather

The clouds

Like grey cotton

Swarming, terrifying

Feel the silence before the storm

The rain

Drizzles turn into a downpour

Lashing, drenching, cleaning

Away the muck

Monsoon

Impending Storm
(Photo Credit: Lakshmy Menon Chatterjee)

Ashes Turn To Dust

What use is your wealth?
It cannot promise health.
What use is your conceit?
It will only bring defeat.
What use is all the fame?
It cannot prevent shame.

Your ashes will turn to dust,
Seeping into Earth's crust.
What people will only see,
Are your deeds, your legacy.
Always try to do your best,
And let God finish the rest.

Cross Culture

When different cultures meet,
The result can be bittersweet.

In the beginning, it is good,
They enjoy diversity in food.

Then the cravings begin slowly,
For food that is more homely.

When wedding plans are designed,
Both customs are kept in mind.

When a child is finally born,
The parents are usually torn.

There is usually contradiction,
To decide the baby's tradition.

The conflicts are at times about,
Whether to take out or dine out.

To overcome these differences,
They have to take some chances.

They both have to mutually agree,
To handle disagreements calmly.

The child should never suffer,
The effects of a mixed culture.

Children should be instructed,
To consider all cultures sacred.

Then only will there be unity,
More friendship and less enmity.

The Race

That gold medal, the claim to fame,
Top of the class, ahead of the game.

The desire for that shiny blue ribbon,
Being the first is always a given.

Failure is rejection, victory is a must,
Even at the risk of losing others' trust.

We continue to covet that what is not ours,
We seek to achieve much greater powers.

A shiny bauble, a rare masterpiece,
Another billionaire, ready to fleece.

Profit is the key, so say the leaders,
Exceed your goals, and be achievers.

From the time of birth, till our death,
The race continues till the last breath.

Lakshmy Menon Chatterjee

FRUSTRATION

No More

In our daily struggle for improvement,
We forget the ultimate goal of happiness.
We engage ourselves in argument,
To gain what, nobody can guess.
Nations clamor for more,
Not ready to give in an inch;
They raid, rape, and gore,
Innocents without a flinch.
We shed so much blood,
Thinking we have won;
Just see the tearful flood,
And realize that nothing can be undone.
Why struggle so relentlessly,
When happy we can be indeed,
If we desire judiciously,
And be kind to those in need?
Away with this senseless bloodbath!
"No More!" we must cry.
Let us not wait for the aftermath,
And live to see our children die.

A Dark Heritage

This is the heart-rending life story,
Of a child born into this old tribe,
That followed a practice utterly gory,
That words cannot be found to describe.

She was born in the hot month of June,
To her mother when she was only fifteen,
During the tranquil night of a full moon,
Alas, born to her parents' deep chagrin.

They named her Aisha, 'she who lives,'
But the life that she was destined for,
Never can be described with adjectives,
Never would she be able to find succor.

For this tribe had a special old custom,
An ancient belief that they always upheld,
And followed like their religious dictum,
To which every single girl was compelled.

Her mother had to undergo the same pain,
When she was a wee lass of just about five,
No carnal pleasure did she ever feel again,
Nor any sensual feelings did she derive.

Aisha's mother said the custom was vital,
To uphold Aisha's modesty and her virtue,
She told Aisha the procedure was trivial,
But this sacrifice to her tribe was due.

Her mother did not know this was wrong,
Her memories of pain were all but faded,
She instructed Aisha to remain strong,
As her organs of pleasure were lacerated.

Like a helpless animal sent to the butcher,
She was conscious through the entire horror,
Aisha screamed and ranted at her tormentor,
But they held her down till it was all over.

For days, time went past by Aisha in a blur,
'The pain would go away,' they lied to her,
But for Aisha, the pain remained forever,
Deceived as she was by her conniving mother.

She vowed to put an end to this old practice,
No more would young girls be mutilated thus,
A campaign she started to help get justice,
She got the village women to form a caucus.

Aisha called for a discussion with the elders,
Convinced them of the flaws in their belief,
She quoted as proof their religious scriptures,
And urged the tribal elders to turn a new leaf.

Her struggle got the attention of the world,
Because she had dared to fight from within,
Stories of her courage and wisdom unfurled,
Changing the lives of the women of Bedouin.

Disguised

Nobody told me about these filthy disguises,
Instruments that concealed all of your vices.
I was a child and as innocent as I could be,
In a twisted moment, you had transformed me.

You personified deception in its vilest form,
As the sunlight yielded to the emerging storm.
An abysmal darkness upon my soul did creep,
So many troubled nights did I piteously weep.

You forcefully commanded me to utter silence,
As you continued to desecrate my pure essence.
Under the deceitful veneer of love and care,
Your filthy hands left me in absolute despair.

Trusted friend to my gullible family you were,
But none knew in you, resided a doppelganger.
A horrendous monster that crept out silently,
When my sheltered world became utterly lonely.

But a decisive day arrived when I finally knew,
It was time to end this ugly chapter with you.
With great courage I gathered from deep within,
I determinedly refused to cater to further sin.

Your dreadful anger was palpable and very clear,
You tried to provoke me multiple times and jeer.
But steadfast I was in my persistent rejection,
No more of these disguises, we were truly done.

Years have gone by, but the fears still reside,
Of these disguises that hide the person inside.
Trust is always transient, hope is forever lost,
When a child experiences this sordid holocaust.

Castles in the Air

Amrita was meant to be a strong woman,
Her name in Sanskrit meant immortality,
But she was sent very early to heaven,
Being born a girl was her only disability.

She could have become a cardiologist,
Mending hearts would be her calling,
But her birth created a wild tempest,
Leaving her mother upset and wailing.

She could have built glorious cities,
An affordable house for every person,
But her parents saw only a dark abyss,
Because she could never be their son.

Or maybe she could have been a pilot,
Carrying people to distant countries,
But to society, she was just a maggot,
Subjecting her folks to more penuries.

She would have become a loving mother,
Unlike the mother to whom she was born,
Equally treating her son and daughter,
No child of hers would she ever scorn.

But these are all just castles in the air,
Because Amrita was a day old at death,
She was buried without even a prayer,
A painful whimper on her last breath.

In a land where goddesses are revered,
Amrita did not stand a chance as a girl,
Her parents ensured her head was severed,
Forever destroying this shining pearl.

The Limit

There comes a tragic time
In a woman's burdened life,
That for no reason or rhyme
She gets fed up of strife.

Beneath that veneer of calm
Lies a vigilante in waiting,
She beguiles you with her charm
Beware, she may be seething.

For do not be unduly deceived
By her discernible weakness,
She reacts to what she received
And transforms her helplessness.

A ticking time bomb she is
Waiting for that final minute,
In life's infinite ellipsis
When you cross her limit.

The Makeover

She was a ravishing damsel,
With eyes like shiny black gel,
Her gait like the lonely gazelle,
Her lips like an unopened shell.

He first saw her at the well,
But to her he could not tell,
In love with her he had fell,
A minute without her was hell.

He felt as if under a dark spell,
Feelings that he could not quell,
Finally, he was forced to tell,
Instead, she cursed him to hell.

Wrath in his raw heart did swell,
Insults that he could not dispel,
Take revenge his mind did compel,
Disfigure he would this vain belle.

He then followed her to the hotel,
Waited for her near the stairwell,
Acid in her throat he would propel,
And then bid her his last farewell.

But his plan did not go too well,
Survive she did unlike Jezebel,
Her blemished face now did repel,
The searing pain made her yell.

Revenge in her heart did so swell,
She tracked him to his seedy motel,
And she cut him up with her scalpel,
So that his tale he could never tell.

An unfortunate fate thus befell,
On this beautiful and innocent belle,
She withdrew into her lonely shell,
Until she could bid this life farewell.

'Murder in Moonlight' - Watercolor Painting
By Lakshmy Menon Chatterjee

The Trees of Badaun

In an Indian town known as Badaun,
The trees now have a new purpose.
The nightingale has lost its fine tune,
As corpses hang from tree branches.

These trees once bore juicy fruits,
For children who were wild and free.
These trees are now used by brutes,
Who rape and hang women with glee.

Badaun women have a reason to fear,
They are the victims of social division.
Nobody dares to stop or interfere,
This mindless and unlawful annihilation.

Hope has become a fleeting sentiment,
Trees having more chances of survival.
Law enforcement is just an ornament,
Righteous activism needs some revival.

The trees of Badaun grow in discontent,
Needing to change these bloodied roots.
Time to remove an impotent government,
So that these trees can grow fresh shoots.

Childhood, Interrupted

From the cold Himalayan mountains,
To where three water bodies meet,
This land has stories in abundance,
Of a tradition so bittersweet.

It has been accepted a norm,
As a girl comes of age and blooms,
Elders' eyes see her transform,
And scamper to find suitable grooms.

Her dreams have no other platform,
Her voice is seldom truly heard,
Discarded remains of her uniform,
Lie in the dark corner, tattered.

She does not fully understand,
The excitement surrounding her,
She happily submits to be scanned,
By strangers, at times a widower.

The day of her betrothal soon befalls,
Agreements and money exchange hands,
She looks longingly at cast-off dolls,
As a veil ominously covers her strands.

From this day on, her face is covered,
Her body claimed and forever plundered,
When spoken to, her eyes stay lowered,
Her mind benumbed and painfully blurred.

She stares at the unforgiving mirror,
And recognizes her dead mother in her,
She beats her chest in misery and anger,
Cursing her fate and hopeless future.

Before long, she becomes a mother too,
Her dreams like her uniforms, tattered,
Scattered in the dusty winds that blew,
Possibilities and hopes forever fractured.

Her first-born, an angel-like daughter,
Blissfully unaware of her mother's pain,
Like a goat being readied for slaughter,
History repeats itself again and again.

There are many such girls uncorrupted,
In little villages, far apart and distant,
Whose childhood is brutally interrupted,
For the sake of traditions so decadent.

But there is still hope of new beginnings,
Braver and assertive have girls become,
Battling through stigma, they grow wings,
To break away and build a new sanctum.

Sorry

Sorry my dear husband,
But I have to go;
To a different land,
But I want to let you know.
As friends, we were good,
As lovers, we were not.
I know I should,
But faithful, I am not.
Forgive me, my dear,
I tried real hard;
But I have to go from here,
To meet my sweetheart.
As I look into your face,
So frozen and horrified.
I don't feel the disgrace,
Since you have died.
You wouldn't have understood,
That's why I killed you dear;
I can forget you for good,
And start life afresh from here.

The Bargain

Distraught parents yearn for some sign,
For their daughter is today twenty-nine.

She is educated, employed, and beautiful,
But in getting married, she is unsuccessful.

The search for a perfect match continues,
Negotiation for a suitable groom ensues.

Indian marriages are arranged by choice,
The likely bride has no opinion to voice.

The boy's parents desire the finest deal,
Their demands are at times quite unreal.

A car, a house, a hundred gold sovereigns,
They enjoy driving these severe bargains.

For them, their son is the bargaining chip,
How can people debase such a relationship?

They value the son against material things,
Concerned about what the betrothal brings.

The bridegroom equally lends a helping hand,
By not saying anything against this demand.

The bride's parents are forever at a loss,
They fear their daughter will gather moss.

For the educated parents of girls believe,
An unmarried girl, God would not reprieve.

So they acquiesce to meet the expectation,
In order to attain level three of salvation.

The groom and his parents never introspect,
They have put up on sale their self-respect.

The bargain is struck and settled with cash,
The wedding is managed with lots of panache.

But happiness is only fleeting, not forever,
The parents of the bride would soon discover.

The bridegroom's parents threaten a backlash,
If they are not paid another splendid stash.

The bride's parents are now completely broke,
Their life's savings have gone up in a smoke.

Then the worst of their fears are realized,
As their daughter is found dead, brutalized.

They woefully question what they did attain,
They have lost their daughter in the bargain.

The evil of dowry continues till this day,
But the time has come to strongly say nay.

To Hell With Hypocrisy

Hypocrisy always wears two faces,
One for self, one for the masses.
Hypocrites never speak their mind,
To their faults, they are blind.

Never practicing what they preach,
Being very accomplished at speech.
Politicians, celebrities, beware,
Your actions are under the glare.

If you cannot follow your words,
You might very well be buzzards.
Scavenging on the hopes of others,
Your beliefs are open for barters.

You want people under your spell,
But frankly, you belong in hell.
There is no greater evil about,
Than one whose honor is in doubt.

Let us chase such hypocrites away,
And let unambiguity pave the way.
We need people who walk the talk,
Holding their ground like a rock.

Alice In The Indian Heartland

Alice chose to leave Wonderland,
To visit the Indian heartland.
She had heard tales of beauty,
But instead, she faced reality.

Venturing into the hectic city,
She purchased a hot cup of tea.
Then, as she went for a stroll,
She fell down an open drain hole.

Alice strove to get some help,
Screaming out with a loud yelp.
And then she felt being lifted,
But to only be unduly molested.

Alice felt awful by this time,
She wanted to report the crime.
She went to the police office,
To demand and get some justice.

But the police laughed at her,
And Alice stormed out in anger.
She next approached the court,
But they just wanted to extort.

Alice could take it no longer,
Heading straight to the hangar.
She flew back to her homeland,
The place known as Wonderland.

The Taboo

The blood from the womb,
That life-giving elixir,
Flows when girls bloom,
Causing elders to cheer.

Superstitions take over,
Unjust customs dictate,
Treating girls like leper,
When they menstruate.

Why is there revulsion?
Is society so immature?
Let us banish the demon,
Branding puberty impure.

This blood creates life,
Sustaining the unborn,
Unfair dogmas are rife,
That women should scorn.

God created women as is,
Acceptance holds the key,
Our society must dismiss,
Beliefs that bring agony.

Let us change this tradition,
Change starts from within,
Women, never seek ablution,
For menstruation is not a sin.

An Unwitting Muse

He was on the prowl,
For his next target.
His mind was so foul,
It just seared my gut.

I was new to the site,
No friends to chat.
He realized my plight,
Posing as a diplomat.

He was very friendly,
Coaxing me to open up.
He appeared crafty,
Desiring to hook up.

I did not reciprocate,
Making him frustrated.
He tried to irritate,
His efforts, wasted.

He became too needy,
He wanted to converse.
Took each opportunity,
To show he was perverse.

I had had enough of him,
His antics were obtuse.
And then just on a whim,
I was no more his muse.

Trapped!

When I first heard of you,
I considered you my savior.
You were reliable and true,
My prayers got their answer.

You promised me the world,
A life of unaffordability.
Slowly the truth unfurled,
You were just a liability.

I accidentally used you once,
Used you, again and again.
Ignoring the consequence,
You became an addiction.

I thought you were secure,
Keeping me out of trouble.
But you made me more poor,
Bringing me added dazzle.

I always paid minimum dues,
But interest was adding up.
I was so unable to refuse,
My debts were building up.

I tried extricating myself,
Taking up a personal loan.
Interest, adding by itself,
Remained the factor unknown.

I was just sinking deeper,
I was feeling handicapped.
Credit cards made me weaker,
They had me wholly trapped.

I could not clear my debts,
The creditors came calling.
I received so many threats,
That finally had me fleeing.

I have started a new phase,
Free from credit card vice.
Free from debt-ridden days,
No more credit card to entice.

Cradle Snatchers

They want them young,
They want them pure,
They rummage among,
The poorest of poor.

Having wrinkled skin,
And gnarled fingers,
They commit the sin,
Of being sex offenders.

Promising a good life,
Stalking needy parents,
They seek a meek wife,
Before her adolescence.

They offer a good sum,
That cannot be refused,
Wedding as per custom,
The girl gets abused.

Fulfilling his fantasy,
Ravaging her tiny body,
A puppet for his fancy,
Just one more victory.

She cries out in pain,
But she has no voice,
She protests in vain,
But she has no choice.

She is then abandoned,
By the man she had wed,
She cannot comprehend,
Why he shared her bed.

Her parents reject her,
Blame her for her fate,
They brand her a slur,
And show her the gate.

She roams alone, tired,
Living as a prostitute,
She is finally acquired,
By a firm of ill repute.

She works as a masseuse,
Providing men pleasures,
She faces further abuse,
From her loyal customers.

Then one day he appears,
The man who ruined her,
She uses a pair of shears,
Killing the cradle snatcher.

INSPIRATION

The Houseboat of Dreams

Like most little girls,
Who loved fairy tales,
I, with my red curls,
Dreamed of white veils.

I dreamed of big castles,
Love's first sweet kiss,
A room full of baubles,
A life of marital bliss.

Then I grew up some more,
My dreams became profound,
Gone was the old folklore,
The castles were drowned.

But one dream I held onto,
To meet my prince charming,
Experience a kiss so true,
Under the flowers of spring.

Now, I was older and wiser,
Still hoping for true love,
Though chances were bleaker,
For me to be the ladylove.

Then one day you appeared,
Just like one of my dreams,
With your muscles and beard,
And a passion that steams.

You swept me off my feet,
Like the proverbial hero,
We were like dogs in heat,
Passionate and all aglow.

We wanted each other alone,
To be closer than before,
We took a houseboat on loan,
And sailed from the shore.

And there on the houseboat,
You knelt in front of me,
A love poem you did quote,
The night had turned dreamy.

My dreams are finally real,
I have found my sweetheart,
This houseboat is my castle,
For until death do us part.

Never give up on your dream,
Always keep your hopes alive,
Life is like an eternal stream,
Where your dreams can survive.

Love On A Houseboat - Acrylic Painting
By Lakshmy Menon Chatterjee

Until A Ballad Was Inspired

My love, you have brought enigmatic meaning,
To the mundane world around my existence.
The sun gave light, but was not shining,
Until your exquisite eyes exuded radiance.
Words were purely devices to communicate,
A poet I became with your heart's cadence.
Flowers were just colors on a wild portrait,
Until your sweet perfume banished my apathy.
Time crawled like a limping invertebrate,
Until fate drew us together in serendipity.
Musical notes held me not in idyllic ecstasy,
Until your melodic voice held me in captivity.
Love was an emotion that remained in dormancy,
Until you lit up my life with your presence.
My love, you have brought enigmatic meaning,
To the remarkable world around my existence.

Lost and Found

This happiness knew no bound,
For today I had again found,
A treasure I had sadly thought,
Lost in this life's battles fought.

Those old memories rushed past,
Some of them happy, some downcast,
Of our times together and apart,
Forever etched in my lonely heart.

Searched I have for you for long,
Where the chances could be strong,
Messages I have written to send,
Missed you so much my dear friend.

Hours spent as the clock chimes,
To recount tales of bygone times,
Changes are so many, but so few,
Memories aplenty for us to renew.

'Tis better to have lost and found,
Than it is to have not been around,
Time and distance are so irrelevant,
When this friendship is a constant.

A Birthday Sonnet

A day of joy for your mom and dad,
Many happy memories you have had,
Another new candle today you blew,
Friend, this sonnet is my gift for you.

Wishes and cakes are now pouring in,
Cards and emails from the next of kin,
Celebrations are on the card for you,
A gala dinner is on the itinerary too!

As you reflect on the years of before,
You wish you had done something more,
Time you do have to explore new things,
New life experiences your future brings.

Make a solemn promise to yourself today,
Life is too short, do not ever waste it away,
Do everything that you have wanted to do,
Eternal happiness is what I wish for you.

Visions of Dawn

The silence before the break of dawn,
Leaves hovering in seasonal bondage,
Flowers budding to bloom and be drawn,
To the first ray of light and pay homage.

As the sky turns deep amber in color,
The twitter of birds fills the cold air,
Chirping and chafing at one another,
Their cacophony is a grateful prayer.

Out in the undulating, wide, blue ocean,
Seagulls swoop in to catch their first meal,
Waves illuminated in the rising new sun,
Fishermen cast their nets for a day's steal.

O'er in the mountains on the rosy horizon,
Tears angrily gush from the wistful snow,
Whispers of milky mist ascend in union,
Dissipating anxiously in the ethereal glow.

Down in the valleys of the lush, green forest,
Fawns clamber for mother's grooming touch,
Dewdrops plummet into the expectant crust,
Ripened fruits escape the weakened clutch.

The sun now shines brighter and much higher,
Nature settles into its rhythmic symphony,
Visions of dawn fade into their daily rigor,
Until the next day begins a new harmony.

Dawn in Sunderbans
(Photo Credit: Lakshmy Menon Chatterjee)

Monsoon Moments

Denizens look resolutely towards the bright, blue skies,
Waiting anxiously with aching and parched throats.
As dark clouds finally emerge, there are grateful sighs,
Welcoming the symphony of those thunderous notes.

The first raindrop penetrates the dry, thirsty crust,
Triggering a sweet earthy scent to permeate the air.
I smell the rain before it cascades down in a gust,
And thank God for this blessing with a silent prayer.

The monsoon has begun, washing away all the grime,
Cleansing this earth of impurities and decadence.
The gushing waters sweep away all the sticky slime,
And flowers bloom again with glorious fragrance.

Earthworms wiggle out from under the fertile loam,
To enjoy the moist and bountiful world right above.
They enjoy the green pastures that are their home,
Occasionally falling prey to the hungry turtle dove.

Rivulets start flowing through naturally-carved moats,
Creating a lovely little pool formed at the tiny nook.
Children gleefully set sail their colorful paper boats,
Watching them sway and swerve down a gurgling brook.

The sea is now overcast and seething in abysmal fury,
Waiting to lash itself against the pummeled sea shore.
It does not relent and knows not its permitted boundary,
Forcing fishermen to remain on land and safe indoor.

Umbrellas of all hues now fulfill their purchased promise,
Covering shivering bodies from the rainy and cold spell.
Lovers use the umbrella to steal a secret, forbidden kiss,
As they huddle together before bidding a tearful farewell.

An occasional ray of sunlight breaks and gleams through,
Ripping the clouds apart with a thin sword of shining gold.
A rainbow makes a silent entry for a hurried rendezvous,
Shimmering splendidly in dazzling colors that are manifold.

And I ardently observe these countless, precious moments,
Capturing each and every poignant picture from my window.
I treasure these memories of absolute monsoon indulgence,
Until the next monsoon decides to cast its vibrant shadow.

Marina

Reflecting the horizon,
Undulates, then swells,
Savior to the fishermen,
Purveyor of sea shells.

Frothing at her lips,
Surges, then withdraws,
Guiding force of ships,
Destroys without cause.

Salt makes her essence,
The shore is her suitor,
In his virile presence,
She seduces with ardor.

Every little rendezvous,
Continues without pause,
Her every graceful move,
Resounds with applause.

She can be a benefactor,
Bringing lost treasures,
She can be the harbinger,
When the earth shudders.

Ocean's Infinity (Photo Credit: Lakshmy Menon Chatterjee)

Tribute To My Teachers

Father used to keep telling me,
Teaching was the noblest job.
Sometimes, I would not agree,
Whenever teachers made me sob.

The teachers whom I remember,
Were those who challenged me.
They made me a self-starter,
Driving away any insecurity.

They believed in my abilities,
And encouraged me constantly.
Giving me many opportunities,
To prove that I was worthy.

They encouraged free thinking,
Fostering my ideas to success.
They helped improve my writing,
Enabling me to become a poetess.

For I had not realized until then,
How they shaped my character.
They provided me inspiration,
To always make myself better.

I look back now and I recollect,
The teachers who supported me.
I wrote this endearing sonnet,
To pay tribute to my faculty.

OBSERVATION

The Pain Beneath The Paint

You elegantly poise in humble grandeur,
Your painted face adorned in trappings,
Awaiting the folksong of the troubadour,
Before the curtains reveal the settings.

The curtains rise, you dance with grace,
Your emphasized eyes endeavor to express,
The troubadour sets the rhythm and pace,
As you perform each gesture with finesse.

You are an expert in the art of Kathakali,
You have admirers from many distant places,
But none of them decipher you are lonely,
They only appreciate your different faces.

Your smile is painted, lips are vermilion,
Spectators venerate your glorious facade,
You fold your hands in divine supplication,
Wishing someone hears you other than God.

But none can understand the pain within,
You are not the person who is performing,
You cannot wash away this unforgiven sin,
The memory that leaves you with an aching.

For you had trodden upon others for fame,
Callously exchanged friends for charlatans,
You peddled your soul to attain this name,
You forsook your darling for your ambitions.

You did not grasp the heartbreak you caused,
The sands of time have blown away forever,
Much later you found your darling was lost,
Her broken heart was too frail to recover.

You realized it was too late to love again,
You already denied romance another chance,
All you presently had was this lasting pain,
Your only solace being this solitary dance.

Kathakali Artist As Lord Krishna - Watercolor Painting By Lakshmy Menon Chatterjee

Her Secret World

Geraldine, an
ordinary woman to
many, but she
had extraordinary
imagination.

To others,
she was uninspiring,
but books transported
her into another realm.

The exotic worlds of
fanciful indulgence
became her universe.
And she, its mistress,
goddess, seductress,
and queen.

As evening crept in,
and she had essayed
her roles for the day,
she patiently waited for
next day's adventure.

Terra Donna Awakens

She had remained dormant for long,
In the warm bowels of Earth's core.
She had hoped the day would not come,
When she would have to be awakened.
But her bountiful home was eroding,
She feared that it would be no more.
She ascended to appraise the damage,
Concealing herself in a forest serene.
The frosty air of the winter morning,
Nipped through her shiny armor of green.
But unknown to her, a girl was there,
Observing her in awe and admiration.
"Are you an angel?" asked the child,
Innocent and pure like an angel herself.
Terra Donna, her thoughts interrupted,
Looked forlornly at the curious little girl.
"No dear, I am the sister of this flora,
A cousin of fauna, and a mother to all."
"Your hair is so green!" the girl gasped,
"And your skin is fair like a white lily."
"Child, my life blood is draining away,
Hence the crust of my skin is now white."
"My hair is green because this forest,
Devoid of new growth, is growing on me."
"I love your shiny dress," the girl declared,
Placing her hand on the glossy green folds.

Salty nectar rolled from Terra Donna's eyes,
She said, "It's made from wasted plastic."
The little girl felt sorry for this woman,
And said, "How can I help you dear lady?"
Terra Donna patted the girl's head gently,
And said, "Please do not stop me my dear."
Terra Donna's hands and feet transformed,
New roots piercing the decayed forest bed.
Her green hair turned into dark green leaves,
New trees born as Terra Donna slipped away.

Their Last Dance

This was their last dance of despair,
Hovering in the early garden light,
Their wings ripping the perfumed air,
As they evaluated their imminent fight.

They were both coveting the same thing,
Delectable nectar from that red flower,
As the angry bumblebee prepared to sting,
The hummingbird whizzed around in a blur.

They dipped and soared in rhythmic unison,
Swirling and twirling to a harmonic drone,
As they pirouetted under the rising sun,
Neither noticed the falcon in their zone.

The falcon watched their dance with intent,
Today's meal was going to be rather easy,
Plunging swiftly in their midst to disorient,
The falcon caught both the bird and the bee.

Mischief Accomplished

Like some top secret spy,
I make mischief on the sly.

With something up my sleeve,
I am always out to deceive.

If I somehow do get caught,
I act like I am distraught.

I am always up to no good,
Even if I get tasty food.

When my owner is very angry,
I do my best to look grumpy.

My owner melts like jelly,
When I show my underbelly.

I purr away in contentment,
When I am not in my element.

Ever Watchful (Photo Credit: Lakshmy Menon Chatterjee)

Duty and Destiny

A simple girl who was just brimming with passion,
A dreamer and singer, who had so much vision,
She was a nun, but she dreamed of big things.
She simply wanted to count her blessings.

Then came a day she was asked by the head mother,
To face the world and to help her discover,
Would she be destined for celibacy?
Or would she be choosing a new destiny?

She met the lovely children and their father,
These poor children had lost their dear mother,
She was expected to bring in discipline.
She was meant to be their guardian.

However, the father had made his decision,
He had always wanted order and precision,
He sought to marry this cruel lady.
This woman just wanted his money.

The father and nun had such different views,
They did not grasp they were each other's muse,
He then confessed his true feelings to her.
And she prepared for her destiny to alter.

Though she was bound by duty to serve God,
She renounced the abbey of her own accord,
She had found true love in this family.
She lived with them forever happily.

Stalking Success

She was from a small town,
But she desired the crown.
She moved to the big city,
To become a huge celebrity.

She wanted pearls and fur,
Along with all the glamour.
She awaited a lucky break,
A risk no one would take.

She started losing all hope,
And became addicted to dope.
Then she was offered a part,
If she agreed to be a tart.

She used her body recklessly,
Pursuing fame relentlessly.
She had no friends or family,
Her life had become lonely.

She slept her way to the top,
Nobody could get her to stop.
She achieved all she desired,
But she was getting so tired.

She had admirers everywhere,
But not one who would care.
Sadly, she was finally undone,
And shot herself with a gun.

Being the cynosure of all eyes,
Comes at such a dear price.
Her success, an old memory,
Is just a footnote in history.

The Eagle And The Blue Jays

It was dawn on a fine summer day,
The sun glinting past dry sprigs.
I noticed the nest of a blue jay,
Built from many leaves and twigs.

The mother tended to her chicks,
As the father watched over them.
Surrounded by morning acoustics,
Unsuspecting of impending mayhem.

A shadow loomed across the sky,
Loud shrieks shattering the quiet.
The blue jays heard the eagle cry,
The call announcing the gauntlet.

The eagle swiftly swooped down,
Approaching the blue jays' nest.
But father blue jay was no clown,
Attacking the eagle's exposed chest.

Mother blue jay joined the fight,
And the eagle found it challenging.
Defeated by their combined might,
The eagle flew away, retreating.

Lakshmy Menon Chatterjee

Watching this scene from my window,
I admired the battle I had beheld.
I had enjoyed the spectacular show,
Of how the eagle had been repelled.

Winged Wars - Watercolor Painting
By Lakshmy Menon Chatterjee

The Chase

When he first spotted her silhouette,
Her curves were framed by moon rays.
A cool, spring breeze gently wafted,
Her scent, setting his desire ablaze.

Her exquisite beauty mesmerized him,
He was enchanted by her gentle grace.
She seemed as ethereal as a seraphim,
The time had come to begin the chase.

He wooed her with subtle compliments,
Lavishing on her fine robes and gems.
He took her to the best restaurants,
And afterwards, he recited her poems.

He only had one objective in mind,
To satisfy his raging, searing lust.
He had his entire strategy designed,
To gradually secure her full trust.

His overtures did not go unnoticed,
And she understood what he desired.
But she too was a clever con artist,
Willing to do whatever was required.

She made him ache for her lithe body,
Leading him on with deceptive words.
She had him convinced of her honesty,
Urging him to share monetary records.

He was absolutely smitten with her,
Ready to drop the chase and commit.
But she did not share the same ardor,
Her only objective being to outwit.

He did not know his chase backfired,
For his fortune was now mostly gone.
One fine day, it finally transpired,
That he had been played like a pawn.

Tryst With A Terrorist

His true identity remains hidden,
His intentions were never obvious,
While he appeared a normal person,
His principles were quite devious.

He glided quietly into the crowd,
Nothing about him raised an alarm,
But his head was constantly bowed,
He did not appear to cause harm.

He accidentally collided into me,
Dropping a package in my purse,
Apologizing, he retreated quickly,
Muttering to himself, some curse.

His demeanor raised my suspicion,
But I did not give it any thought,
Then I saw his parcel with a gun,
Causing me to become distraught.

I saw him weaving through masses,
And I followed him with purpose,
He seemed to like public places,
Tailing him was becoming arduous.

But I finally caught up with him,
Shouting the name on the parcel,
Whipping around, his face grim,
He displayed his sizeable arsenal.

He was strapped with explosives,
From his chest down to his pelvis,
Leaving no guesses to his motives,
This madman really meant business.

For a split second, I was frozen,
Watching him clutch the trigger,
Then I wrenched out his own gun,
And killed this agent of terror.

Thus transpired my terrible tryst,
Forever etched within my memory,
A chance meeting with a terrorist,
Who is a closed chapter of history.

Armed To Disarm

Her graceful poise,
And seductive voice,
Made men her slaves,
Until their graves.

Her mischievous eyes,
And convincing lies,
Tricked her admirers,
To remain bachelors.

Her seductive figure,
And suggestive ardor,
Caused men to quiver,
Giving her the power.

Her mellifluous skin,
And her impish grin,
Led men to surrender,
Their beloved treasure.

She misused her assets,
To clear all her debts,
She applied her charm,
Always armed to disarm.

The Downfall Of The Apes

She had seen her friend
With the latest trend
And she wanted to have it too.
She went to the mall
Dressed up like a doll
Now she is looking like a shrew.

He was at the bar
When he saw the car
And he desired it like hell.
He stole lots of cash
Got caught in a flash
Now he languishes in a cell.

Mom treasured those rings
All those diamond things
And she liked to deck it all up.
She splurged on big gems
And those diadems
Now she is begging with a cup.

Father loved the suits
And those handsome boots
And he did not have any care.
He bought many toys
Like those giddy boys
Now he has no more change to spare.

If you love to ape
You cannot escape
The lure of things you cannot own.
You cannot deny
You live a big lie
By trying to become a clone.

Fame Is A Fickle Mistress

Sharda had dreamed of success,
She was an actress of finesse.
Though she was not at the top,
She was more than just a prop.

Then occurred her lucky break,
A role she could not forsake.
She acted her part flawlessly,
Getting accolades universally.

She was the epitome of grace,
Becoming the celebrated face.
Adorning most magazine covers,
She wielded charismatic powers.

Dethroning the reigning star,
Not even one opponent to spar.
She had achieved the pinnacle,
Leaving aspirants to struggle.

Her arrogance and complacence,
Created more foes than friends.
She thought success was forever,
A lie she would soon discover.

New faces began replacing hers,
Her fans dwindling in numbers.
She found she was not the queen,
She had been replaced by a teen.

The fame she cherished was gone,
Forfeiting the highest echelon.
A new starlet has now ascended,
As Sharda's hopes lay discarded.

When The Hunter Becomes The Hunted

You crouch silently, observing,
Your stealthy eyes appraising,
The object of your fascination,
Grazing without any trepidation.

You slip into the freezing water,
Paddling across the winding river,
Your eyes fixed on your dear prize,
A beast follows, you do not realize.

This beast with cold, yellow eyes,
Takes advantage of your surprise,
For it lives in both water and land,
Forcing you to take your last stand.

You may be the lord of the jungle,
But today you fought your equal,
A rare occurrence forever charted,
As the hunter became the hunted.

Hunter Turns Hunted - Acrylic Painting
By Lakshmy Menon Chatterjee

Traitor

Treachery was in his blood
Blood that burned like acid
Acid thoughts that caused chaos
Chaos brought on by his ethos
Ethos formed from past events
Events that triggered dissents
Dissents that inspired hatred
Hatred made his soul go putrid
Putrid actions meant debauchery
Debauchery became treachery
Treachery was in his blood...